DATE DUE

FREE UNION

THE

POETRY
SERIES

Free Union

POEMS BY JOHN CASTEEN

The University of Georgia Press   Athens and London

Published by The University of Georgia Press

Athens, Georgia 30602

www.ugapress.org

© 2009 by John Casteen

Set in Minion Pro by Mindy Basinger Hill

Printed and bound by Thomson-Shore

The paper in this book meets the guidelines for
permanence and durability of the Committee on
Production Guidelines for Book Longevity of the
Council on Library Resources.

Printed in the United States of America

12   11   10   09   08   P   5   4   3   2   1

Library of Congress Cataloging-in-Publication Data

Casteen, John.

Free union : poems / by John Casteen.

        p.   cm. — (The VQR poetry series)

ISBN 978-0-8203-3328-1 (pbk. : alk. paper)

1. Virginia—Poetry. I. Title.

PS3603.A8745F74 2009

811'.6—dc22   2008037206

British Library Cataloging-in-Publication Data available

for Laurie

Contents

Acknowledgments   ix

Poem for Mary Magdalene   1

I. FREE UNION

Free Union   5

Murmur   6

Meditation at Backbone   7

In Lambing Season   8

Summer Wages   10

Shaper   11

Plant Life   13

Tinnitus   15

Gravid   16

Fiat Lux   17

You Leave One Room, You Enter Another   18

Units of Measure   19

A Dictionary of Flowers   20

I Forget Myself   21

Insomnia   22

Regret   23

For Those Who Knew Her   24

Disputanta to Zuni   25

Lens   26

Enormity   27

Night Hunting   28

Pausing to Sharpen Tools, I Recall a Line of Russell Annabel   29

Shad Roe   31

A Portrait of the Artist as an Old Man   32

Insomnia II   33

II. MORE ABOUT THE WORLD OF THINGS

AND THE WORLD OF IDEAS

More about the World of Things and the World of Ideas   37

Sestina on the Change of Season   38

The Honey War   40

For Our Next President   41

Cold on the Shoulder   46

Chording   47

Silver   50

Chain Song   51

Close Work   52

Letter-Poem   53

Polestar   56

Thanksgiving   57

Empiricism in November   58

The Gift   59

Spring Poem for My Mother   60

Like a Lion in the Winter   61

Out of Season   62

Letter to Family, before Leaving   63

The Night Pasture   65

Notes   67

Acknowledgments

The author would like to thank the editors and readers of the following journals, where some of these poems first appeared:

The Blue Moon Review: "Silver"
Electronic Poetry Review: "Gravid," "Shad Roe"
The Georgia Review: "Disputanta to Zuni," "Plant Life"
Iowa Journal of Cultural Studies: "Out of Season"
The Iowa Review: "Murmur"
Meridian: "Chording," "A Dictionary of Flowers," "Enormity," "For Those Who Knew Her," "The Honey War"
New Orleans Review: "The Gift," "Insomnia II," "Polestar," "Sestina on the Change of Season"
Ploughshares: "Night Hunting," "Shaper"
Poetry Daily: "Plant Life"
Rivendell: "Empiricism in November," "Free Union"
Shenandoah: "Insomnia," "Meditation at Backbone," "Poem for Mary Magdalene," "A Portrait of the Artist as an Old Man," "Summer Wages"
Southern Poetry Review: "Spring Poem for My Mother"
The Southern Review: "Close Work," "You Leave One Room, You Enter Another"
"Night Hunting" was selected for *The Best American Poetry 2008* by guest editor Charles Wright.

My thanks to Gordon and Mary Sacks, Mike and Lisa Marshall, Dick and Nancy Kennedy, Peter Bowyer, the late Jim Bowyer, Mike and Lauren Funk, Harry Bruns, and Bill Baker for the many kindnesses they have shown me.

And to those who brought me along: Debra Nystrom, Dave Smith, and James Galvin. I am especially grateful to Charles Wright, whose sense of poise and rigor is a continuing inspiration: *ars longa.*

And to Chuck Brown, James Brown, Bootsy Collins, Rick James, Aimee Mann, Bill Monroe, Tony Rice, Earl Scruggs, Doc Watson, Clarence White, and Meg and Jack White, who show the way.

And to those whose care and guidance made this work possible: Matthew Kirsch, Sam Witt, Mary Szybist, Andrew Smith, Nathan Englander, past and present members of the Earlysville Literary Society (The Poets of E'ville), Dave Lucas, Ted Genoways and Mary Anne Andrei, Frank Chang, and especially Elizabeth Casteen, my sister. And to my family, especially my mother, Sue Selden, Dick Selden, and my father, John T. Casteen III.

FREE UNION

Poem for Mary Magdalene
John 8:7

I was raised to be the judging kind.
Not much halts that, not much galls it,
but the winter sun stalls me. Sedge-color sedge,
black Iowa River, north of town, tan marsh-grass,
black trees above the river. The hard bluffs,
ice shelf eight inches off the river ice,
crowned fissures—*he among you who is without*
fault, I know, I know. Was raised on order,
and faith, and ecstatic witness.

Diffuse sun that shines on machines left to weather
and on babies just born in hospitals and on cities,
on saltsacks hung on lowest limbs
in the apple orchard: the hands of the world
have thick nails, blunt tips, chapped backs,
black callus. What work will they not will?
Ice storms on Afton Mountain leave the mountain
effervescing for days. Two cardinals preen
in a boxwood hedge. Below, in thaw,

Tye River clears its clear throat, ice slurry
from the falls spreading and bobbing. Dad's story ends
with an upturned nest of fingerling copperheads,
flood-orphaned, beautiful and hazel, writhing blind
in new shoots of grass. Not much is irreplaceable;
not much, but some. In idle hours,
whose surplice is dust, the treeline's
Braille sentence above the riverbank reads,
thanks for noticing, return to your labors.

I

Free Union

Free Union

Again, the cataclysm of landscape:
my Blue Ridge, collapsing into creamy hayfields
in the valley. To the south, Break Heart Road.
Slam Gate Road. White Hall, and its lines
of orchard trees as nets cast to agree with the grade.

I'll try again. Redtop grasses,
never knew their real names,
with Buck Mountain purpling and clairvoyant
hung Calder-like above. To the north,
Bacon Hollow. Horsetrailers crawl along
to Amicus. Barns like churches. The indifferent,
the iridescent ridgeline. Espaliered plum trees.

What the hell. All I can say is nothing.
Free Union, Virginia: the husk of the general store,
broad semaphores of six-board fence.
The frieze of the hills, and of their omnipresence.
The hawser of the tongue, and its knots:
sheet-bend, bowline-on-a-bight, easily tied,
as easily made loose. Ends whipped tight in windings
of paste-waxed cord, linen, against unraveling.

Murmur

I've always had this hole inside my heart;
it's literal, and every two years needs
machines with cords taped onto me and plugged
by nurses with their gelid hands. In truth

it's never caused me trouble, or not much.
I need my prophylaxis certain times,
like anybody; don't much mind gray eyes
of residents who promenade to see

(or, rather, hear) my fault when I'm laid out
for show. I'm clinical; I'm teachable.
They have to use their stethoscopes like men
on subs use pings to find the enemy.

Have always been ventricular, septal, and defective
to them. Which suits me fine. I like to know
they squirm when asked to pin it down, and watch
my small systolic-diastolic cycles misfire

on television. Every time there's that suck
and whistle, leading to the next, referring
to the first, which speaks to the last. My own
inefficiency. The exegesis white-coats try

and try to learn: my fast, off pulse. Heartstutter.
Like murmured things old women said at cards
when I was small: *Good night,* they said. *Great day
in the morning.* And, *Lord, Lord. Lord have mercy.*

Meditation at Backbone

September now, a new moon, everybody tending
to their grain drills, repacking the bearing,
filing the burr from the spindle; everyone wishing
they'd taken more risks, or fewer. The Lord giveth,
they say, and He may or may not take some back.
I knew this would happen again, this impatience,

this wish that when the dust rises
from behind the combines I'd also rise,
and gradually see back over my life, as though
it were Mercator-projected out below me.
It might just be these cool fall nights,
or it might be mortal fear; if I knew

I'd tell you straight. In silage sheds
the difference between a patch and a field
is curing. Old women trail the harvesters and trucks
across the plain because those ears are free.
But nothing's free, and the lone tree's leaves
too few this fall. The tree's going to die, and anyway

who gave us to believe all this would pass
for passion? The fences are ticking and need
mended, quick. I pass between a rail and stile
where any ewe could go. Things are falling
away beneath me again, like an out-of-body experience
Mike told me once he'd had: he saw the souls

of those he loved as spheres, floating, glowing
like there was a light inside and the lights were him.
I made a box for him, rock maple, signed it inside a joint
and said, *keep that story here for me, I'll be needing it.*

In Lambing Season

I've got to make my strong run now,
　　　　I've got to be awake
to everybody's yard-trees exploding,
　　　　forsythia like a grievance
against winter, piquant edible citric
　　　　redbud flowers quickening.

Living things all seem entropic and motile
　　　　and strike while the iron's hot,
the stale cold world pleased to welcome new blood:
　　　　there, in someone's side-field,
dicey little half-steps, half-lookarounds.
　　　　They waltz solo timed in fours.

Ziggurats of hay attend them, and the smell
　　　　of earth turned off
the mouldboard plow and disc harrow.
　　　　The cutting of it;
the cleaving, then the stitching back down.
　　　　You can't give it all

away, can't get it all quite back,
　　　　each personal history
like recounting a natural disaster
　　　　(everybody knows
you say one right thing, you forswear
　　　　right others; it isn't all

one way), like process-variable interactions,
  like margins of error.
What lies within the photograph's white borders:
  that quarter-inch tells not
what it contains but what it frames,
  language's little slur,

elision between the real and the retold.
  A bit slips by
like paper boats on fire, like little paper boats;
  I think in Wingina
we could release them, they'd tack noiselessly
  around the Hardware River's bends

and on. Each an idea. Most people behave
  irrationally most of the time.
Right? But that's not all I know on earth,
  nor all I need to know.
Further: one's life built as a communal residence,
  manifold smallish rooms

communicating along one long central hallway,
  all their doors opening out
onto the sensual world. Who is still sleeping?
  And who has gone:
once was myself a plowboy, and a shepherd of sheep.
  They're someone's else this year.

Summer Wages

Good bet things won't come through, seems like,
like they usually don't. The screaming saws
were in my dreams again, the building dream,
but when I woke my hands were silent.
Late winter, and the sky a damp blanket, you remember
what isn't there: cumulonimbus marching along
eastward, tumescing and detumescing, stacking themselves
up on themselves, say nothing, say everything.
What is it to be alone without loneliness,
to understand the self as one person walking
in circles that get smaller and smaller? Like you're coins
draining down those funnels they put in places
where someone needs money and kids watch them go.
Before they fall they make that pawl-and-ratchet sound
and there again's the saw-squeal, the worm-drive,
the green fir, the project, the drawing board seems like
we're always going back to, the eight-lights, the gone summer.

Shaper

In the days when I was training
on the Griggio in Blaise's shop,
all metric and fabulous, with dials and rings
and a brake, electromagnetic, meant
to simplify setup (it didn't), I was always
wrangling against the power feeder, trying
to keep straight what was cope and what
was stick, how to run cock bead with the face
on the fence, whether to bolt the tenon clamp
on the ball-bearing table before or after
I pinned the miter gauge in place.

It was crazy-making. I loathed the machine
as I had loved Thorn's simple, elegant
Powermatic of Delphine Avenue, Waynesboro.
I'd get all shaky and gun-shy and couldn't stand
to have to fix the shaper steel between
the lock-knife collars and tweak them
into their perfect little circles of scotia, bolection,
astragal. But what I did like—this

is the thing of it, finally—was that the cutterhead
was so big, and the column of air it started moving
so massive, that simply by opening one's mouth
and moving the lips in and out in larger or smaller shapes
of O, one sang with a voice not one's own, and whistled.
Like blowing across the neck of a bottle, but weirder.
It was as though a harmonic existed in the back of the throat
along a string drawn tight by the work of the shaper:
to remove whatever is not the thing desired of it,
the carbide cutter, after all, formed in the shape of matter

one can do without. In the end familiarity
bred contempt, and my fear, which was vast,

gave way to convenience: nothing bad kept happening.
We turned out acres and acres of frame-and-panel,
and I got paid my wage. Still always played
the mouth-game, even after the wonder of it,
and the oddity, blew away like so much swarf
through the dust-pipe, down the cyclone, to the drop-box,
filling bins and bins and bins and bins and bins.

Plant Life

What I remember now about that place is dust, and words
we know for all its kinds: the Root borer's tailings; swarf
from corrugated shaper-steel; colloidal, gelatinous masses
of slake like accretions in caves in the Altendorf cabinet
and the wide-belt sander. *Timesaver* is its name;
a man on the nameplate is pulling the hands of a clock
in counterclockwise motion, as though a Rodin ran the shop,
as though the motes of dust that boil and whorl away
from the hairs of our arms, from the coarse fabric
of our work-shirts, have something in them of art.
And coated in it, all day in its Brownian sluices,
as newborns cloaked in cauls of vernix, but cherry red,
at day's end: the long line of us waiting our turn at the air chuck,
the blowing hose a cipher of the common weal.

Us unloading flatbed trucks like ants with boards.
I think of Freddy Dawson on the rough-milling line,
my nose is seven, right-hand ring finger half-missing, him all glue
and 3-in-One oil and chips from the gang ripper
and upcut. And Donnie MacDonald's incisive way, pointing
with his sanded-sharp pencil, as if he held an instrument
in his hand, as if it were a caduceus hung behind him
on the wall, not the time clock, not the wing-saws

of the stack dado head. My foreman, the Sage of Elkton,
balletic with his fingers in the air: the drawer-reveals, so.
The tenoning, so. Who alone best knew the panel router's story
sticks and how to tweak the Unipoint to truth.
In heaven all the lumber's lovely, time is not money
and we can always steal a moment in the breeze
we're just shooting; the angle-wheel of the variety saw
locks top dead center at a flawless, impeccable ninety.   13

What else? In heaven we can all afford Starretts
and to buy the stuff we build. But here, as it were,
as it is, the sole of the other safety-shoe falls
in step with the hydraulic flattening-bar and chain
of the clamp-carrier; you read the paper and hot-box
in the john, you cultivate the soul in days of face-jointing,
weeks of the old pull-and-slide on the dovetailer,
months of squaring diagonals of doorframes
at assembly. Time passes quickly. There's no excuse.
And dust is what you have inside and out to show.

Tinnitus

It's all right there, in purples and in greens
dogmatic in the fauvist smarmy flier
my doctor keeps around for guys like me.
I knew the drill before I ever thought
to go, but here it's all spelled out: she says
cumulative, says *the highs go first.* And grackles
in the side-yard, beaks like scissors cutting,
gave me yesterday what proof there is.

I never know what I don't hear, you know,
by definition: P.E. is in the house
in full effect and shooting lessons
I got paid to give. And am reminded how
in Wendell Berry's country way he asks
what we can know: a limit of perception
shows itself in guesses, and conjecture;
we're looking out the backs of yards the mind

can map, and at the night's tarbucket mouth.
This ringing in my ears (the symptom is
the cause) stays with me like a friend
I hate. I'm thinking of the way some flutes
of crystal after rinsing ring like bells
and truth we think we hear; forgive
my little parlor trick (that zeugma's all
I mean). Oh, God. Am I already gone.

Gravid

In this which is the season of invented errands,
the least of tasks explains a drive along the smaller roads.
We live in two instincts: the one to make ready,
the other to rest, and wait. The baby was due
yesterday. I painted trim in the guest bath
and hunted squirrels with my cell phone on. The trees
are late this year and vivid, and we are one month
without rain. It does favors for our apples, this weather,
and for our gutters, which need mending. I have in mind
to use the stock I made for something in the freezer.

So: pearl onions, venison roast, parsnips, fennel bulb, thyme.
Laurie says the whole house smells meaty and I think
she means good. We talk about a trip we'll take next fall,
we talk about auctions, we talk about the fear of death.
The logic seems trimesterly and incomprehensible.
The baby's room is ready, and aired out, and bright.
The garden is gone to seed and I am calling all over
for kind people I haven't seen in years. They seem fine.
I'm thinking of my child's introduction to this world,
or to its unambiguous, its relevant: sweet, sour, bitter, salt.

Fiat Lux

Leaving the hospital, sky freaked red,
with you still there: it seems
implausible, as though my life
has distilled into a small radius
inscribed about your little body.

The trees above the reservoir
are luminous and changed.
Early morning, and blue leaf-smoke
from the Old Rag fire choking
Charlottesville and cloaking us

as though in fog. The fires burn a week.
We all are burnt and fragile
with strain and no sleep. I hold
your head from falling back, late
these past nights, and flatter

myself: the nurses do all say
you take after your father.
One shows us the finger trick.
One, how all new ones hate to be naked.
Onto the shores of the new world

are we washed, and as those
from whose eyes a veil has been lifted.

You Leave One Room, You Enter Another

Year after year, this: first warm days (March:
young shoots: the verdant palette, again) and the two-track
side-hilling Buck's Elbow Mountain; it's liturgical.
I drive by the church-house that straddles the brook,
drive by the fork where they set free those bears
who nuisances make of themselves in the park.
I seem to want to say one fixates on the small,

the immediately-at-hand, the repeatable,
like declensions of dead-language verbs;
like the particular blue of the chicory-flowers
who volunteer anew each June. Saffron color
of unmown ryegrass, wintered over, in slant-light.
I write this hard by Grover Vandevender's store
where Faulkner and my father met

to ride the trails from here to Barracks Stud.
Called *Barracks* for Hessians who garrisoned there.
By this same line of cedars. Where I live now
all's freighted, and never done. Here, one's best
ambiguities: the senses in which one is left
when one's choices are lifted away. Keep looking.
Foothills' lockstitch, knit and purled, knit and purled,

this landscape like a suture laid by shaky hands;
here I am tightly held, and new, and not healed up.
You leave one room, you enter another, world without end;
I could not live in books alone or spend my life in grief.
There remain of course those greens that collards are,
the greens they aren't; the several worlds we inhabit.
The more than several. We have the never the less,

and we have the never the more.   18

Units of Measure

So many rods, so many chains,
this dram equivalent, that gauge of wire,
what number screw (and which pitch?
and Acme thread, or York? is it the coarse-
or fine-thread tap?), so many hands.
The sum of stones one is. The cetane count.
A hogshead of tobacco in long tons of holds.
Inches of mercury; atmospheres; millibars.
And the cubits of one's breadth, or myths
we hear about the rule of thumb,

its nature. And this is what we do:
and's also what the ruler does:
we take a thing we think we know
and hold it up against the real,
and say we thus have its measure.
But: the ambivalence of the unit;
its arbitrariness. How we made it all up.
The opprobrium of diamonds to the carat.
We are that platinum bar in France,
are but that meter sealed tight in its vault.

A Dictionary of Flowers

Little taxonomies of loveliness, their names
like explanations: *jonquil,* you are invited; *iris,*
we're serving avgolemono; *dahlia,* inside of a week
a conflict will at long last resolve itself.

The past flickers on like pleurisy.
I hardly know anyone. The poster child
of virtue; no. Worse: of benign neglect.
A shirker. The upholsterer's organdy work

in the good offices of one's attorneys.
A dictionary of flowers is a register
of metaphor, with which it is co-populous.
And, *calendula,* have you seen our friends?

Never to be a carrier of tales, or to dissemble.
Genuflecting in my sleep beneath the starry sky.
I don't have any unfinished business here,
just this one diurnal dissatisfaction: middle

of the day, Darjeeling tea with sugar,
buttered toast, boiled farm egg, salt
and I'm a problem lunch won't solve.
To feel oneself affixed to the hull of a planet

and wheeling, wheeling, like murders of crows.

I Forget Myself

I went to clear a fence and found
three things: First, the job increased
in size the more of it was done. Then,
the fence grown through young hickories,
its rusted wire swollen through their trunks.
Third, a way to pass from yard to woods
without the architect's grand plan:
edge-scrub undefines edges, blurs them.

This is a poem about still being young.
Just Thursday night, no great occasion,
no hinge on which to make the wide door swing:
in my heart I am one dog walking in a field,
and I am another dog sleeping by the stove.
So sometimes I might use the words;
sometimes I might just leave the words alone.
Or might reach up and give grapevines a shake
or might concede. They'll always win.

What I think about is the ability to make
everything stop, to halt that other, inner weather
whose fronts roll through the old two-dogged heart.
Do we receive the moment of clarity or do we
invent it. Do we raise up our hands
to hide from the embarrassment of not knowing.
Do we say, oh. *Oh.* Forgive me. I forget myself.

I thought you were someone I knew.

Insomnia

These nights, and the self steps out of itself,
my dad tapping his leg while "Earl's Breakdown" spins.
Like Miró. The old guys worked like Miró,
primitive instruments and the same power:
background of rare color, the lead parted out
on top of it. On the porch of the mountain house

two months ago I could've said forget it,
it's whiskey talking, but Earl Scruggs got it dead
to rights and never missed a note. Carr's Ridge:

scuppernongs, and red oaks wave and shift and a buck
uphill flashes. I'd threaded him ten days before
and followed sign, left corn and carrots to bring him,

just to look at, and he showed. We don't much stand
on ceremony, men and animals, around there; he heads on,
and I say a line of poetry for my father, and now I think

about that, a night-drinker of milk, while not sleeping.
We're told that once seeing was believing, that
there wasn't all this creakiness between word and thing.

Then between the world of things and the world of ideas
what's left is sweet sap flowing in sleepless hours, xylem
and phloem, vocabularies that char, nomenclatures that say

themselves and stay so we remember: kingdom,
phylum, class, order, family, genus, species.

Regret

This life, it is like conducting
the symphony of a warring country;
the cellist has been shot through the wrist it's all in,
the horn player has buried his child
and sworn off music.

The conductor will never hear his piece as he hears it.
Sometimes I wake between three and four, these winter nights,
clenching tightly the what-is-not-there,
and I can't negotiate with that kind of failure.
Outside the wind is roaring at the house.

I had to throw away someone I loved.
That thing that I said at first, about the conductor?
Such a man has no cause to expect redemption.
Fine. So I'll never understand anything.
So this life, it's never going to explain anything.

For Those Who Knew Her

I'm told she stood a long time on the spot
she was meant to be buried, that she weighed it
against others, and looked this way across the town,
studying the full far view of the Blue Ridge,
which way the wind overtook that hill,
what flowers might arrive between the road
and the old tall cedar. I'm sure it was her girls
that she was thinking of, what kind of place
they'd find her staying in, what they would ever see
as they came to remember her. Consider
the kindness, and the choice. That was her way.

Disputanta to Zuni

Pulp and coal, long trains and anything grows.
Drop silos rust by the Southern States, and combines
drip anhydrous down the rows. Black stalks of cotton
gone woody, their bolls floating above like heat-shimmer.
We are out of the drought, we think. All's green,
and the five flat fingers of the sweet gum inch
over the guardrails along 460. A plasma cutter
formed the press-broke wheels of heavy trucks
whose chromed lugs spin bright orbits by my window;
we have crossed to the south side of the river, the soil
a different color, alluvial, the continent divided
into plots of peanut, feedlot, soy. The packinghouses'

clerestory windows over corrugated high ceilings: the building acts
like a smokestack, has to draw right. And the sibilance
of stock-fans, of radials: like seeing stars, that noise,
or like what one hears underwater, the clicks and shrieks

that bubbles make when someone kicks or we go hypoxic.
Or like an exhalation when we reach the certain strictures
we find ourselves within. Again: chinoiseries the planter leaves
by sticking to the contour of a field; they pass so fast

we see them in that we see only an instant of them,
editing what we can't get all of, get enough of. Always
in the middle of one thing, at the edge of something else,
always moving on. Disputanta, Waverly, Wakefield, Ivor, Zuni:

what might living here be like? Like no one does.
Like I don't already. Like I'm living anyplace else.

Lens

In these hot close nights of Virginia's summer
I like to take a chair beneath the anvil clouds and cricket-hurry
of the backyard, I like to see the off-blue flicker
and glare in my neighbor's window, the television on;

it must be a comfort, a respite, the cathode-ray tube
a reminder of some program or other they saw once.
It's pretty. *You make me want to be a better man,* I think,
as Jack Nicholson tells Helen Hunt in that movie

where his character can't quit failing people. He's most hopeless
just after he shows her what he could have done, have been.
In a photograph everyone likes, our daughter is standing
in this grass, her face visible, but amplified, distorted

a little, through a soap bubble my wife had impressively blown
and that floated, like a sphere set loose upon the cosmos,
like an iridescent clear ball of shot across the composition
I was trying for. It's something in her facial expression, her mien

—she is eighteen months, if I remember right—that wants
to know *what was it I was trying to think of?* her upturned palm
reaching out as if to ask the little world what it had to offer;
she seems to have achieved that state of universal envy,

blissfully, singularly unaware of her own limitations,
disabused of the notion of her own mortality, fierce, fearless,
incredulous that such a thing as a transparent globe could pass
before her, like an aleph, and oscillate, and then flash off.

Enormity

I have lost more than I kept.
My father encased in amber,
staring out of his life at me.
He can well recall himself,
I fear.

One more white-sky July day,
piedmont of Virginia; I have lost
nostalgia. The food is here,
the waitress says: duck breast,
grilled endive. I feel a fool.

Our garden fails same time each year.
I say good-bye to it. The weeds say
nature abhors a vacuum: what is filling me.
Our life here is poor and full.
And what's left: the good and bad one thing,

always to be alone, and
always looking at yourself.

Night Hunting

Because we wanted things the way they were
in our minds' black eyes we waited. The beaver
raising ripples in a V behind his head
the thing we wanted. A weed is what might grow
where you don't want it; a dahlia could be a weed,
or love, or other notions. The heart can't choose
to find itself enchanted; the hand can't choose
to change the shape of water. How strange, to hope
to see the signs of motion, to make an end
to Peter's old refrain: *He'll be along, son of a bitch,*
and then you best be ready. So sure, and so sure
that when he shines the light the thing will show
along the other shore. What next? Well,
you've killed animals before. Invited here
for company in the cold night, and because
ever handy with rifles. What next is wait
and see, what next may be the lone report, the ever-
widening circles, blood-blossom, the spirit rising slow
like oily smoke above still waters. We wanted
a pond to look like a pond: standing poplars,
shallows unsullied, fish and frogs and salamanders.
The gleaming back of fur and fat may not belong,
or may: God of varmints, God of will, forgive us
our trespasses. We know precisely what we do.

Pausing to Sharpen Tools,
I Recall a Line of Russell Annabel

Beside this bench I built, tall windows stand and all
they hold: indices of taps; dies laid flat in their drawers; Silver
and Deming drills by the letter and number. Green eyes
of my small daughter; the boiling clouds. Beyond, two Staymans,
four Winesaps, *Diospyros virginiana* and the rest

of the world. To see it is to hear its sound, its cry,
like the keening of a febrile child, like a person
without choices. How like a father; how like that child.
How like the eighty-eight named constellations
we circle and flicker, circle and flicker. At three

my girl can tell her satellites from stars, the way
the blue-/redshifted spins all give themselves away.
She likes to see the wan half-moon in daylight; it keeps
a banker's hours, arrogating to themselves what is
the chattel of another. I like to think a scythe is meant

to take its name from how it sounds at work: *sigh:*
when it's all about its subtractive chores. It frees
thick sheaves of stalks at each long stroke; they're bound
in shocks in photographs and dreams. The heart's about
its own subtractive chores, late at night, in rooms

a dog walks through alone while people sleep,
breathing in, breathing out. I wonder about that
sleep-shudder, that twitch one executes while falling off;
I want to know just what it wants to tell, and whom.
Now, here: once more bent at the lap-and-hone, the grind

and true: paring chisel, mortise chisel. I make a mirror
of their backs. It's a gift. I think of the sawyer's rough errand,
slabbing flitch after flitch off the white-oak log
the carriage carries past his blade; it's good, I think,
to watch him box the heart and peel away

whatever lacks the bull's-eye at its end. Like peristalsis,
that job: Head saw. Trim stand. Creosote tank. Crosstie.
That's a good hour's work. That's every bit of an hour.
But fate didn't love us, Annabel says, about weather
or something, and I'm reminded of the obvious way

beyond a certain age one has to quit that trick
with the lit match popped in the O of the mouth,
the lips a needle's eye the fingers thread. It lacks a certain
dignity, that trick, and onlookers' sharp inhalations
gasp against but do not quench the fire one consumes,

the curlicues and twists of smoke that leak away
from the corners of the mouth's dumb smile.
*When I was a child I spake as a child, I understood
as a child,* this with me, too: *now I know in part;
but then shall I know even as also I am known.* How odd

to turn to First Corinthians when people wed. To say
not knowing one small thing's the thin end of the wedge,
the razor edge, that part which has no width. Euclid spoke
the truth bare as this bare patch on my hand's back, and I'm
finished, I'm ready to resume. Fate doesn't hate us, either.

Shad Roe

There was one apricot, in Connecticut: sublime.
Two martinis with fried chicken in Saratoga, 1999,
when the McIntosh apples were coming in.
Potomac River oysters my grandmother fried—
this was Christmas—a man in the Navy Yard
had tonged them that morning for my uncle.
Also: Laurie's potatoes, bluefish we caught
and grilled, Smithfield ham, garden tomatoes.

But last night, after everything, the bacon, the parsley,
the lemon, so fragile: old Bruns had brought in some shad roe.
I cannot attempt to describe the flavors, except to say
I felt the roe abscond with each remembered pleasure
I'd ever had. My father said it was as he'd had it
as a boy, and I think he meant right: it had that single,
Platonic, implacable rightness, the mark of the divine
in the physical world. (You have to really love food.)

Like the peregrination of the single idea, the
in-this-am-I-made-whole summation of scattered things.
Louis asks *are the pleasures of ironic detachment*
less deep than the pleasures of true affection? I fear
that, yes, they may be. I am thinking of last night again,
now, and the set of my father's jaw as he leans his head
to one side, deciding about the first bite. (You have to get
a little bit of everything, you know, the first bite. Then

pick and choose.) We roll our eyes to one side to remember,
to the other side to lie. Between the purely reclaimed
and the purely imagined: firm, slim, kidney-colored
taut little lobed loaves, twice-savored, twice-revisited.   31

A Portrait of the Artist as an Old Man

A sign above the door says you are a stranger
here but once; the old man is stooped in the yard.
He has his hands thrust in the ground.
I'm thinking *this is harrowing, this is cultivation.*
He looks down at the hands and is reminded.
His whistling sounds from the kitchen, "Salt Creek";
he's biding time, studying the joining of joists.
His shirt is blue, his bones are brittle, there is water
in his eyes. The animals are gone; he doesn't miss them.
Old work-clothes fat with lanolin stand for themselves.
An old letter, in an old box: *I have always taught you,*
it says, *to spit hard on the ground, and tell anybody*
go straight to hell.
                    He's dreaming now, it's night:
the smell of ether in the carb. Lights of freighters
running south down the bay. Trunnions indexed
in races, close tolerances. *A dull tool is an abomination*
before God. On the sill plate, between dark ladders
of lath, there's an old pile of blunted razors rusting
slowly, sealed in the dark. He's counting to ten
on his fingers, joyous, again and again and again.

Insomnia II

Acer saccharum, Juglans nigra, Pterocarpus soyauxii.
I came in from outside and made and ate black stew.
Some people can be content with small acts with
small consequences but winter doesn't stay
like nothing doesn't. Which cavils the weather we love

to talk about, and to outlast. Like figures of speech.
Like a rip on the horizon. I painted myself into a corner;
I owe a debt I don't know how to repay.
Late this week or early next, put the clutch in,
take the clutch out; I'll forgive a lot about a person

if they love the same things I do. Here, James River
runs green, rocky, and clear. Here, nobody can be unhappy
when they get what's coming to them. Where's it coming
to them from? Lay the hymnal down, and get your act
together, boy. Hold one of your gentle hands with the other.

II

More about the World of
Things and the World of Ideas

More about the World
of Things and the World of Ideas

Like he didn't know better. Sitting there
outside in all kinds of weather. Once
I saw a gang of turkeys wheeling over the James,
their wingbeats percussive and bright,
the grainfields above Howardsville luminous
beneath the river-trees. The whistle and spray. Who is
the patron saint of birds and rivers.

We learn that there is the word: *fiat*,
say, or *truth*. And then there is the world.
Do we learn the one without asking of the other
what is it. Do we say, whither goest thou, then
there go I with thee. I think of Ash Wednesday,
people streaming forth from church, marked
with the thing we're all meant to remember:

There is, after all, that other world, where
our letters are nothing. Where we can know the truth
but cannot write its name. Here, then, is the anvil,
warm from its celestial forge; here is the hammer,
pealing like a bell. Our words the wrinkles in damascus.
This is recollection, and is the pattern behind the pattern.

Sestina on the Change of Season

Each year when things turn green I see the loop
of swallows there in someone's barn, a braid
of old tobacco hung away from light and contact
like a ham, or like a sign, for who would care
to taste of it (*afición* is patience) in early spring
before its flavors had their fair chance to turn?

One knows that each fine thing must wait its turn,
remembers that the bottom of the loop
will dry and feather, coiled tight as a spring,
when time is right, the four tastes' braid
made quick and lithe for those who care
to know it. It's a small thing, but a contact

point of inherited knowledge, a hinge, a contact
lens one sees time passing through as seasons turn
and reel. And then those swallows, spooling without care
for life or limb; they're reckless, out of the loop
of knowing how grim actuaries will upbraid
one's wildest hairs when sap is up and spring

expounds. That *hurry*; the sense that one should spring
into action, pierce the veil, make human contact;
I'm thinking of the girl my wife once was, the braid
of her hair, the way she would surprise me at each turn.
I play that back in soundless and in endless loop
and am amazed at what we learned of lust, and care.

There are those clocks one tends with passion and with care
("gravity escapement"), governed by the tension of a spring
that time unwinds with pendula and through a loop
of cable on a roll; the gears make contact,
or something, and the hands, turning, turn
one thing into another, time into potential, braid

of swinging clockweights' rise and fall, braid
of what we give (as time demands) our love to, and our care;
these warm rains plash and roll across the terne
our roof is seamed from, which again each spring
reveals the little black and sorry spots of contact
with leaf-fall. One sees one's life as through a loupe,

blurred-out at the edges, and not the care one shows a loop
of negatives; the braid of faces on the contact
sheets half-turn, half-smile. As waters from a spring.

The Honey War

*Van Buren County, Iowa, February 184_*

Because we all had our minds on death
and taxes, we never thought just to move.
We all stood there, looking wanly up at the sky,
mouths hanging open like at the movies
when the deal is really going down, and history
overran us, overwhelmed us. We were stuck, forever
in the present, forever imagining ourselves
as other than we were, what we still are.
But how do you make God laugh? You tell Him your plans.
The cartographers convinced us of nothing
we didn't already believe, and already we'd cast our lot,
all of one like mind, and all fighting that sweet war.

For Our Next President

Who understood the need for compromise.
Who grew up not having and not having
to contend with his own potential.
Who figured he was fine like he was.
Who was penny-wise and pound-foolish, who knew
to feed a cold, starve a fever, who robbed
Peter to pay Paul, whose mouth
stayed tight shut unless eating or speaking:
he of the shaking hands, the kissing babies,
son of the nation, child of ideas, who wrote
nothing but always read what he'd signed, fear
for him. Who bit the bullet, who kept
his old knife handy. Whose bootstraps
are darkened from much handling. Who smoked
with soldiers and read the great books in college
and plays all hands close to the chest.
Who was put off his feed for a while by a sorrow.
Whose January should have been cake, but.
Who always never got out much and
from whom the meek shall inherit the earth.

Who was smarter than his own problems.
We all knew he was headed someplace since always.
Who broke with his fellows in favor of a higher end.
Who could force his detractors to eat crow.
Who was at some point overtaken by grief.
Whose transgressions were duly noted, but
regarding whom tact required a willful avoidance of issues.
Who stood by his people in famine and plenty.
Who kept his own counsel and stuck to his guns.
Who was selectively brave and circumspect.
Who neither bore the lantern nor kept the vigil,
but to whom others looked when they sought guidance.
Who kept in time with the seasons intuitively.
Who was clean. Who was thrifty. Who saw
what needed doing and delegated accordingly.
Keep this man at a safe but reachable distance.
Who maintained a steady and consistent belief
in the conditions of sin, and even from an early age.

Whose concern was the fifth column, the wooden shoe,
the third estate. Who saw his intimates
as liabilities, even to the point of suspicion,
whose expressions of love stuck in his craw,
and who was, finally, a cripple. Whose idea of order
presupposed the partial abnegation of self.
Who had fished crappie as a boy under the bridge-abutment.
Who had eyes of obsidian and translucent motives.
Who was stable. Who will maintain, who will lead
the lambs to their slaughter, who never once stole.
Who understands joy as a means to an end.
He troubleshoots, he's a fixer, why
does the idea of him so linger? Why
can we not simply erect the statuary,
forsaking the man? Because we are alive in him,
who is the all-seeing eye atop the pyramid.
Who rode a wooden train down a wooden track.
Who is the linchpin, the clevis, the keystone, the hinge,
the cipher, the wheelman, and the sounder of depths.

Who made hay when the sun did shine.
Who wore it in, wore it out, made it do
or did without. But who'd fix what wasn't broke.
Who was given to believe pride would prevail.
Who brought contingencies to the fore.
Who was a creature of habit.
Whose insurgencies are whose street riots.
What shall we do? And how shall we live?
When the decline of an order leaves only
the knowledge of how-to. Who read and believed
we have seen the best of our time.
Who uncouched his own rhetoric,
and could speak little while saying much,
discretion being the better part of wisdom.
Whose shortcomings are all temporary, like ours.
Whose odds are all surmountable.
Who snarls in the face of adversity
and graciously, without rancor, leads the charge.
Who'd gone to catch the falling knife.

V

It's like déjà vu all over again.
Who maybe wasn't perfect but who knew enough
to blend what ought to be with what is.
Who lost sleep over the smallest distinctions.
Who gathered information obsessively
and from impeccably credible sources. Who kept tally
of his own preferences: pinwale over wide,
burnished over chromed, coached over schooled.
Stay the course, he reminds himself. *Mind
the larger principle, stay your hand, let the details
see to themselves.* Who chose to be rash
when rashness was an advantage. Who forsook
himself in his own time of need, raising others
where he could have been raised up in their stead.
Who knew the bitch payback was, or ought to be.
Whose logic is the logic of the magnet.
Whose faith is the faith of the firstborn.
Whose needs are the needs of refinement.
Who traffics in madness when the world is mad.
Who recalls the caissons and rifles and is made whole.

Cold on the Shoulder

It's true. Mountain acres are bigger.
The television tells me it is raining
at my home. Here I predict the weather
by the lay of the fur of a dog, no joke,
and the width of the spirit level's bubble.
But what about that other, inner weather?
The spare room has the sphagnum smell
of young plants, things growing. It was this
involvement that I wanted. Wasn't it?
Someone must have lost the photograph
I remember someone took: it's me
as a kid, tired in the face and happy
standing at a cornfield's edge before a line
of dark oak woods, crescent-shaped
scope-cut over the right eye, before
the bruise came on. *I was with you,*
the eyes are saying, *before you were with yourself.*

Chording

There is a density in the air that smells like nothing,
   my body stiffening after coffee like a wire,
the only promise the lick of color in the speaking trees—

from the fire tower I watched the wind push the lake
   like spread fingers reaching into themselves,
then by the shore walking, and the sodium traces drought leaves
   on stones in the sun. Ashes over fossils.
      Tall pines hung over the water.

Finally, immersion, a laying-on of hands, fingertips on the face
   and early fall, far north, the light changing again,
my compass shifting. All the fall things—acorns falling,
     agate sound of lapped rocks,
     the finally-flowering weeds—carry away uphill

to the houseful of people making themselves hard to love,
   not hearing the wind touch the pines, then untouch them.
The trees preen. Clothes on a line are stragglers
   waving from behind, voices clamped in wind, hoping
     to sway the eye of the lone swimmer.

The reach to the island is a small life
   of its own; it leaves the electric tinge of the drying air
     to finger the late flowers, then leave them.
     The bees are gone, the heat is gone, the house is up the hill
       and it may be my house. The island looms,
        and I must be there.

II. CERTAINTY

I don't like empty houses,
no one in the kitchen and at worst leaves
    blowing through an open door—
I don't like the idea of old people being alone,
    or remembering things I said. I once knew a woman
        grown so tired of people
    she drove a fence post deep into the ground
        and told all she had to tell to it instead.

Fall here is the flaming trees singing:
    keep warm, settle in, the lake's turning over,
        your shoes are on your feet, and go on

III. FOR DOC WATSON

Song, not ideas about the thing, but the thing itself,
    four chords and fingerpicks and probably more
miles than I'll drive today in my father's Cadillac, godfearing
    G-run strung across the soundhole I carry
in my head and can't not hear in the small hours,
    then tired in the car, rolling—

Dulcimers and woodsmoke breeze across the place
    Tidewater has become—an array, a pattern
of boulevards with the names of victory. The tides breathe
    up, then secede. My granddad knows the price he paid
for which year's Studie, first by far with a postwar car,
    even here in Chesapeake, Virginia, home
of his tools: a wrench for a valve on a mothballed sub,
    drift punches holed up in racks,
        the grinder that snatched his hand away.

Doc, today I drove east from the mountains to the sea,
　　your sweet drawl pure Carolina and clean
　　　　as the pinch-pick's rasp on a flat spruce top—it sings
　　　　　　as gears move, dust sinks
　　　　　over the city sprawled along the floodplain, tomatoes

hang on the vine and my ears ring
　　　as though someone had spoken
　　of me someplace else, without the hum of the power lines,
　　　　without all that rose-colored singing.

IV. HOMAGE TO MERWIN

　　It's the seldom-sensed, the rarefied flat light rising
from the loins of the animals of fables, telling us what it is
the carrier of ladders knows, *Nachträglichkeit,* that we can know
　　a thing and also not know it
　　　　in the same moment—

　　that song rises like fumes within us,
　　　　that the air whistles not litanies
　　　of what we've heard other people say,
　　　　　but of small birds

　　in whose birth we take no part—the ring of hammers falling
　　　and falling, men speaking to ships with light
　　　　　from towers by the sea.

Silver

Of all the poems I've ever wanted to write,
there's one that has the honey locust blooming,
its thorns still green and malleable in late spring,
the lilt of its flowers strewn across the yard.
This is not that poem, though here in the old house

whose heartpine floors wane at each corner
I can imagine it. That poem will only arrive
when I'm done with house-raising, done with thrift,
done with the blue bowl full of buttermilk
soaking venison I dressed with Peter in the fall.

That poem will arrive only when the two bands
of woven silver are finished, and all the music's
been played, Peter and Dale have gone home
to their wives and sons, and the floor's swept:
I want to wear one of those rings, to give myself

to the poem when it arrives, to have
the light slanting across the floorboards,
maybe rain on the way, the dooryard in order,
the wind finally rising, the choosing not to.

Chain Song

I crank back on him though he haul
my shoulder's socket loose, he strains
and drives until the bent rod's cold steel butt
wedged up in my teen crotch strikes
straight home and my knees numb.
This blue hooked deep on tube lures runs
dark fathoms under Plum Gut's high chop, piles
of froth and spume where currents parry;
I yank straight up the bone plate palate,
two-ought shortshank solid locked there,
his shard teeth shredding the surgical bait.
This bastard could pull stumps I heard some old sot
say once who lost his finger's end two joints
to a blue, and so what? For him, for them
the crabpicking women of Tangier sing, and
for our lithe prey. Prescient, Pyrrhic victory:
I hoist him up and out to heave his lights
as though bright gills might breathe, and he
deflates. Indignant catatonia seizes him all through;
I gut him clean and quick and you're proud, father.
For this radiance. For this one, hard, uncoiling blue.

Close Work

It's getting on for fall now, coming to the cold
    I recall, the rented house, plains town,
   during the weather season, the rafters shifting
under the wind load. The sashes rattled, the blinds sighed,
    my father told me on the telephone
     his wife was leaving him.

Soon after, he came here. We sat on the bed, we talked
    to Virginia on the telephone. I saw
   his glance snag for a small moment across a photograph
     ten years old propped on the nightstand.
    He's leaned against a wall in Vienna, looking
     toward himself, now, in my house.
Earl Scruggs is on, winter drawing down, fog atop the hills:
    the line is the sugartrace in the maple.
     And I think the word is *chatoyance,* the light
      through the window, his eyes on his eyes.

It's clever, I think, how cicadas return.
   Clever poplars, holding fast to the stream-sides.
   Clever how annealing tool steel makes the colors of flowers.
    Back home the cattle cars say nothing, ever,
      but Southern Serves the South.
    Because the heart is a valve without a governor.
     The house is full, and it's just us two.
      Rich and dark as humus, the fact remains.

Letter-Poem

I still love the winter woods,
   rime on the weather side of the trees,
      hung limbs old ambitions
         their trunks forgot.
  In Maine last spring three days came
    when the beech trees all put out their leaves—
  the livid, the singing green explained, finally,
    this, yes, is what all that weight was for.
I'm thinking of Virginia's coal trains banging down
    past Mike and Lisa's farm from Rockfish Gap
      from the coalfields at Hinton down
  to Hampton Roads, past restive pastures, seam to sea,
      seam to sea.
    The diesels shake the ground, shake our houses:
      half the smoke we get to see is steam.

          ◦—

When Bill Baker got out of Furman,
    his father gave him a beautiful big Guernsey
      and a note to build a house on spec.
  Here's some good advice he has,
      good if you can take it:
    If you've got time or money, take the time.
In these woods north of town,
   the bluffs above the river suggest I watch
   late afternoon reach trees' gray trunks
     through light snow. It is easy to believe in this light
    I taste smoke in pears, easy to believe it may suffice
    to simply be honest and kind,
      to believe I may provide good tilth.

But these are different from our Southern woods,
  though not by far. These lack
our dogwood, scrub oak, mountain laurel,
    the red clay and the shale of the hillsides.
  These woods are all burls and spalts,
      larches with wrong leaves.

Because he loves me, my father
  wants me to know what he knows
      about the way the world works, and I don't.
I become more and more like myself
  than I ever was, like my father with hands
cracked after sawing one day; these are his father's
    hands, now full of pain,
        full of prayer.
  The woods are full of widow-makers, full of squaws,
    and I wear my father's clothes
      when I wear my father's kind of clothes.
  Advice. Like age it stands to reason,
      one of the few pure things
        we fail to forget.

          ⌒

  Apartment window, Iowa City,
watching the chemical planes return
    on their paired pairs of wings.

At this writing it is six weeks since
  I've been at the farm, eight weeks
since Mike's steer (cut a little proud)

charged on us, three days
      since Lisa's arrhythmic heart event;
         I hear she's on the mend, their girls
      with her mother. The line's staying busy.
         This, not miles or days
            of driving, is what distance is.

   I've been planing the sashes
      and mullions for my house,
         lately, in my mind.
   I've dovetailed and drawpegged
      the kingposts to the sleepers,
         raised the gambrels from the summer beams,
         nailed the sapling up for topping-out.

   I'm thinking again of my family in Virginia
and how our closest places close. My flowers are sent.
      My blessings circle like those redtail hawks
         riding thermals up the flanks of the Blue Ridge,
            looking, looking, not moving,
               not gone. Not so far gone.

Polestar

I didn't mean to make the train
jump off its tracks. But one time I was in a fight
in a cold locked room with wooden walls
and I realized I was trying to kill someone—
but more than the green light of dusk,
more than the lolling, broken neck,
beyond a prayer, beyond release I needed
the high blueshifted wane of the polestar
to sound the half note that means go.
I wanted to be a simple machine.
High in the cold woods, alone, I know
you saw down into that spinning
place behind my chest where rage was.

Now in the night on my back
on the shifting, heaving mirror of lake ice
that speaks up to you with its groans,
I lay clamped between two flat sheets
that match with no seam: I let up,
I let his collar go, I turned my fingers loose
from their knot. Mercy, fall now.
Bury me with an acorn in my mouth.
The beacon moves a little on the ridgetop
each night, so the seasons are changing,
the light shifting along the shoal it marks.
I unscrewed and stole the lockset from the door
to every house I ever lived in.

Thanksgiving

Lose an hour in the morning,
you'll be all day hunting for it.
But Peter never hunts mornings
and never drinks hunting. Last night
our clothes, rinsed in rainwater,
hung out off the porch, away from where
things smell like us. Something about that
departure from the human, that distance,

makes days walking under red oaks differ.
Say something that ought to mean something,
then say something else; I prefer woods.
To carry peppermint in the pockets,
laying up at midday by the lower field
where deer cross from cover to cover.

You can glass the treelines all day long,
actually; that's what Peter's father does.
But you see more walking, and it hurts
the knees sweetly at night. That's the thing:
I don't want to die because I don't
want to stop feeling pleasure.
It's that simple, some days, especially
in fall, hid from the senses, seeing things.

Empiricism in November

This is the promise of fall: Peter and me, walking
    with our rifles and jackets away up Carr's Ridge
to hunt deer rising from fog in the valley. Late afternoon:
    Tin pines. Tin oaks. Early evening: Sassafras smell,
light oil, woolsweat. Cold smoke sinks in rain from pipes
    outside. All year long I hold the loaded gun

on my downhill side like I was told. The promise is true
    like dowsing is, no point not believing. Iron sky color,
my shoulder hurts like a voice I can't place, like the sudden,
    receding *I* . . . of the .30-'06; this world reflects
against the way I see it asymmetrical like any face
    and like my own. Inside one room says to the next

looks like he got rode hard, then put up wet; my hands shake
    like water, sullen in whistling pipes. That's instructive.
What's compelling is the loam smell, the fractal bursts
    of the tree-crowns, and their directness: good cider,
for example, doesn't taste like apples. It tastes like cider.
    Peter's father watches. He knows a couple tricks,

been down this road a time or two before. Been all along it.
    I am twenty. He's holding the picture of us going.

The Gift

Beyond Mike's cattle-gate, the field is nothing,
    the sycamore less than nothing.
Pippins bend as Baptist bells carry from town,
    a mile. Beneath the house
        is a crate of nails,
    and every nail's a perfect nail. Look at one.

The dogs are learning to be careful
and attentive and run circles around reason.
    It's fall, so men are shooting back the bolts
        of the beautiful rifles.
    As I write, the range of variables narrows.
    I think, the line is like the seal of the manifold

to the block, most correct when least visible. Diesel mules creep
  in switching yards, their lights on night and day.
  Mike had said his gifts to me would make me
  more useful to him: A tape. Level. Framing hammer. Fence pliers.
  Five Acres and Independence; Lives of the Poets.

Cold coffee, cold comfort, the moon just past new
and waxing, there's no need for challenge, nothing to break
    the fall of leaves as squirrels go nuts.
    I have spent my time standing between field and road
        wishing I was drunk and waiting
      for something to change my life, which it won't.
The dog's warm, wet—healthy—nose pushes up
  my free hand, the hand I don't have
  on the chain latch. The bells ring and ring.
      I open the pipe gate;
          we populate, we punctuate the field.

Spring Poem for My Mother

It isn't simple, Mother, what brings you to your knees
in your own backyard, scratching red clay for the broken
pieces of other people's fifths. It's finding something to show life
has happened here before, and you're returning to yourself, pregnant
with me, scrubbing floors for comfort and for a promise

coming true now. I took six tons of junk from this yard
to the landfill, for a clean start. There's no such thing,
but the grass is nice. I was barely off the milk and then
you went back east; I don't remember really but people
have told me about it. Like many children I don't care

about the details of anybody's divorce or their marriage, either.
I say I don't care because now in your new house
and yard your orbits are lurching to stops, though moons
keep waxing, filling, waning, newing. I'm glad you've got
a plot to till, rhythms, lives you can watch again and again

growing, as you watch part of mine one single time.
It's not simple, there are circles within circles within
what your body knows; this is reason, or what
you were right to call reason, and it's dazzling. Now
the tight crocuses arrive, and they're yours to watch, to hold.

Like a Lion in the Winter

It's the obvious again, early morning in February, far north,
    haven't seen thaw in a dog's age till eastern light bears cries
of cedar waxwings on the winter-apple in the yard: in the early melt,
        the birds skid in crescents between branches, the fruit
           sun-softened or hanging like stones in the shade—

It lasts the morning, then the sheen of glare
    on the lake-ice hardens back, the basin fills with trucks
        and men. We're all afternoon with augers
    in the city of smeltshacks in the cold sun,
        baiting crows with junk fish—

I'm seeing bright with liquor and sunlight, head frozen,
    laid out on the ice with the winter-apple seized to my mind
        again, the heavy branches wetting, lifting,
    then frozen again, peripatetic, birds fleeing,
        then the tree a new tree, not the one it had been—

In winter Maine's a beaten zone, fired upon
    from all points north, the noise of rifles in winter
        saying *learn to love the shadow of your legs*
    the moon throws on the lake-ice, learn to be alone
        without loneliness, to let the self fix on what it will—

Sailing on the sea of the cold, my heart is a ship
    laden above all Plimsolls: in the night, after the thaw,
after fishing, I shine a beam up from the yard. It picks the clouds
        over in rows, discerning, a still tunnel of light
    vignetting the storm we'll see tonight,
birds already fed, winter tree static, content, the front looming—

Out of Season

Late November and the first snow a glaze of nothing
    on the tamaracks and the young pines
walking for deer or for walking with the gun
    a sound scrapes across the frozen ground
to me, silent as possible, easing among the boughs
    but again the lick of sound I've never heard
like an axhead levering free, creaky but urgent
    then a rash of rust, slack tail dragging
head low to the ground, eyes hung low and swinging
    then Mike *a fox you see in daylight's a sick fox*
and running now, she turns, turns, eyes flat and I follow
    with the bead dead on her, Jesus, Jesus, thumbflick
it's not possible, the gun bucking up, roar returning,
    her jerking down, me shaking like rain and I'm sorry
when I bury her the blood steams a hole in the snow
    and I want to know what she knows
            the fever and the light

Letter to Family, before Leaving

If I don't see you, go to the poolroom
and tell Kenny Morris when he gets out of jail
I turned out all right. Tell him me leaving here
is like a stone sinking in water,
it's a natural thing, and I'll settle.
I haven't been to the farm yet
but in our back field there
a horse-drawn mower's rusting
in the way that old things do, left to themselves.
Over in the orchards on Wayland's place
there's a cider house older than I know;
when I pick there I think how weather
beats on what you leave in it and how
if I stayed out long enough I'd wear
like those planks and dry strong as them.

People truck-farmed Mike's for years.
When we burned a thirties oak barn
ten years fallen back by the mower,
junk trees that grew up in it blew boiled-sap
steam like kettles and our faces scorched
even twenty feet from the burn-pile.
Raking down the ashes showed the stone
foundation of the place, tight and square
and not a dab of mortise in it to've cracked.
Penning sheep I hauled for him
I bent more nails than I have words
in my mouth on another old barn there;
what it takes, Mike tells me, is a perfect series
of perfect strokes, which no one ever gets.

When the peaches come in at Wayland's
watch the summer light on the twisted trunks
of the trees. Walk in the front field
I bush-hogged and hear the grass rush
under your boots: when it comes time to hay again
this field will miss me, will also miss

who rode that other mower before
I drove Mike's Farmall in wind
dry as the sheaf of winter wheat tacked up
in the barn, reaped when they still sowed it.
I hope I never tire of this valley's changing faces,
smaller roads wrinkling my affection
across its beaten cheeks, and bringing you,
family, my life, my love.

The Night Pasture

No road leads there. We walk
a different way each time, as to a still,
lest bootheels' beaten trails betray
this darkest field to prying eyes
or to our careless own. We near and its echoes
threaten through dense woods, a secret passed along
by underbrush: keep back, come this way.

The night pasture is that place we keep
when possible in the mind's back forty,
fenced by what we allow memory to allow;
it's that neglected corner where we saw our lovers lying
to us, where we caught our mothers in the act,
where we saw through the television's idiot gray eye
ourselves. Its wild grasses feed the frantic animals
we keep and cannot countenance.

There is no safe containment there. Our herding
of its staring beasts is a joke, not even therapeutic.
No pen breaks them. They feint from around corners
of streets, from old favorite shirts, from gesture;

in the night pasture sometime before dawn
this morning, a calf died whose head I'd guided
through the uterus and out. The heifer's lowing
had long since stopped, the bugle of her body's knowledge;
I believe she'd felt her calf's heart quit, just like
she'd felt its breech-birth hooves coming down
and begun bellowing. Little changed, except something
sank in me like a leaf settling silently in water—

there's another mouth to feed, but I think
you know where. I've said enough about it now.

Notes

"Poem for Mary Magdalene": It is an idiosyncrasy of usage that my family says the names of rivers without an article preceding them; the word "river" functions as a surname. The reference in the last stanza is to the story "Notes from the Flood," from "John Casteen: 16 Stories," special issue, *St. Andrews Review*, no. 21, 1981.

"Meditation at Backbone": Backbone State Park, Strawberry Point, Iowa.

"Tinnitus": With thanks to Public Enemy for their show at Trax, Charlottesville, 1992 or so.

"Gravid" and "Fiat Lux": October 29 and November 4, 2000.

"A Dictionary of Flowers": For Sam Witt; February 27, 2003.

"I Forget Myself" and "Cold on the Shoulder" borrow the phrase "inner weather" from Robert Frost's "Tree at My Window."

"Shad Roe": March 2000, Charlottesville. With thanks to Harry Bruns of Howardsville.

"More about the World of Things and the World of Ideas": Statue of Saint Thomas Aquinas, Alderman Road, Charlottesville, Virginia.

"The Honey War": When Iowa and Missouri were territories, a cartographer's error left unresolved the provenance of a long, wedge-shaped area south of what is now the border between the two states. Honey was the only sweetener available to the settlers, who for several years fought border skirmishes for the right to harvest it from hives in the disputed area. The joke in this poem is Marvin Bell's.

"For Our Next President": The device that drove the composition of this cycle owes much to the work of Jim Heynen (specifically *The Man Who Kept Cigars in His Cap*, Graywolf Press, 1979, and *You Know What Is Right*, North Point Press, 1985) and to Allen Ginsberg's *Howl*. This poem was a product of the 1994 Iowa political primary season.

"Chording": III: In 1943 my grandfather lost three large patches of flesh on his right hand to a grinder whose tool rest had been left loose by a previous operator. The lost flesh was replaced with skin grafts from his upper arm, which are still clearly visible on his hand. He was outfitting the interior of an aircraft carrier in the Norfolk Naval Shipyard. IV: This passage refers to John Keats's letters to his brother on negative capability.

"Letter-Poem": For Lisa Marshall; February 1995, Iowa City.

"Like a Lion in the Winter": Hoyt Axton. The "beaten zone" is the berm behind the targets on a rifle range.

BOOKS IN THE SERIES

The History of Anonymity
Jennifer Chang

Hardscrabble
Kevin McFadden

Field Folly Snow
Cecily Parks

Boy
Patrick Phillips

Salvinia Molesta
Victoria Chang

Anna, Washing
Ted Genoways

Free Union
John Casteen

Quiver
Susan B. A. Somers-Willett